If I Wer

I'd End All

the Pain

Struggling with evil, suffering and faith

Also by John Dickson:

Hanging in There

A Sneaking Suspicion

A Hell of a Life

Simply Christianity: A modern guide to the ancient faith

If I Were God I'd Make Myself Clearer

If I Were God I'd End All the Pain

Struggling with evil, suffering and faith

John Dickson

SYDNEY · YOUNGSTOWN

Special thanks to:

My many mates who have kindly allowed
their stories to appear in the book.
Dominic, Chris and Rachel for their suggestions,
many of which they'll recognize throughout.
My beautiful family (Buff, Joshua and Sophie)
for enduring the 'suffering' caused by my long hours
absorbed in the writing of the book.

For Brian, Judy and Debra,
in memory of Mandy.

If I Were God, I'd End All the Pain
Third edition
© John Dickson 2019

First edition 2001
Revised edition 2002

Matthias Media
(St Matthias Press Ltd ACN 067 558 365)
Email: info@matthiasmedia.com.au
Internet: www.matthiasmedia.com.au
Please visit our website for current postal and telephone contact information.

Matthias Media (USA)
Email: sales@matthiasmedia.com
Internet: www.matthiasmedia.com
Please visit our website for current postal and telephone contact information.

ISBN 978 1 925424 62 1

Cover design by Judy Dao. Typesetting by Lankshear Design.

Contents

Contents

Introduction

The problem with writing a book on 'evil, suffering and faith', apart from the sheer magnitude of the question, is that you appear to be saying you have the answers. Surely, if you write a book on a topic you have to be something of an expert! Otherwise, why should anyone bother to read your work? I am really dreading the interview where I'm asked, "OK, so what's your answer to the question of suffering?"

Over the many months I've been piecing this book together, I've decided that an 'expert' on the problem of pain is something I am not. My strength—if it can be called that—is in my capacity to *doubt*. There is hardly a belief which others hold sacred that I have not at one time or other seriously questioned. Some I have rejected forever. I don't know if this is due to a religion-less upbringing, a suspicious personality or just plain pride, but for some reason I find it difficult to believe in something strongly if I have not spent time doubting it just as vigorously.

So, whatever else this book represents, at its heart it is a tribute to doubt. Nothing has exercised my sceptical muscles as much as the issue of human pain—mine, yours, that Kenyan baby with AIDS I'll never meet, and so on. I look at it all and find myself wondering: "If I were God, I'd end all the pain, so why doesn't HE? Is he powerless? Is he not interested in us? Or is he just plain not there?" The questions—some philosophical, mostly practical—begin to mount.

This is not to say I don't attempt to answer my own questions—I do. In fact, that's the beauty of doubt. It forces you to sit loosely enough to your 'beliefs' that you can begin to look at them objectively. It makes you investigate, search out, and once you're done, either to stop believing or to start believing with fresh conviction. Both of these outcomes have made their mark on the pages that follow.

Let me begin by telling you where my doubting faith began.

1

The last one standing

The front page of the *Evening News of India,* Tuesday, October 12, 1976, ran the following story:

> All 89 passengers and six crew members were killed when an Indian Airlines' plane, bound for Madras, crashed within minutes of take-off at Santa Cruz airport, at 1:40 am, today. The plane… was only some three minutes airborne when its pilot… noticed a fire in one of the engines. He was reported to have told air traffic control of the fire, and… said: "I am coming back".
>
> Eyewitnesses, including friends and relatives who had come to see the passengers off… saw the plane burning in the night sky, like a red ball, before it crashed. The passengers had no chance.

I remember that night well. I was watching TV—*The Sullivans,* I believe—with my two brothers, Rob and Jaime. The phone rang. Mum answered. It was the news she'd been dreading ever since she heard the midday radio bulletin. "Mrs Dickson", said the nervous voice at the other end, "I'm afraid I have terrible news…"

Dad was on the plane.

The days following are a bit of a blur in my memory —I was only nine years old—but my mum recently told me that I approached her a day or so after the accident to ask: "Why did God let Dad's plane crash?" Mum can't recall anything of what she said in reply. Ours, like so many modern Australian homes, was not 'religious' by any stretch of the imagination: we never went to church, never attended Sunday school and, as far as I can remember, never even discussed spiritual issues. It was a stable, loving home, but one completely without God. Nevertheless, somehow, as a nine-year-old boy, I still held the conviction that the Creator was meant to be responsible for keeping the world together, and on this occasion he had mucked things right up.

This is a feeling shared every day by thousands and thousands of people, some of whom experience a level of pain and tragedy most of us will never know. Every time a marriage is betrayed, a business collapses, or a child dies of cancer; every time a country is bombed, a flood rages, or a famine decimates, the cry goes up: WHY?

There is no point denying the force of this question. Indeed, despite the confidence I may at points exude in a faith-based perspective on evil and suffering, I want to confess that my own faith is not untroubled by this question. I feel deeply the weight of the problem that suffering presents, and at times I still find myself asking, "Why, God?" I am not sure that the Bible—the main source of my perspective—answers all of my questions, let alone all of yours. It will soon become apparent that my own view is not that the Good Book presents a complete and final explanation for all evil and suffering—far from it. However, I think that it offers the best explanation, the *least incoherent* one. I cling to the Bible's perspective not because it has some 'knock-down' argument to offer, but simply because, to me, it appears to be the only perspective which is not itself knocked-out by the force of this age-old question. It seems to be the last one standing.

That's why a large part of this book will be devoted to outlining several other approaches to this question. My intention here is not simply to criticise other points of view. By comparing and contrasting the alternatives, I hope to show how the intriguing and beautiful nature of the biblical perspective on suffering is the best one on offer.

But before I explain how other traditions under-stand suffering, I want to say something about how the question before us is often put. Sometimes it's phrased as a logical proof against God. I want to show briefly that this way of arguing isn't successful, before I deal with the more important issues of suffering and faith.

Does suffering disprove God?

A friend of mine is a Qantas pilot and one evening as he looked out of the flight-deck window at the thousands of bright stars in the night sky he said to his first officer, "Look at that. It's hard to believe there's no

God." The first officer quickly replied, "Not when you've been through Vietnam and seen the violence I've seen". My mate changed subjects.

Essentially the argument suggests that the presence of evil in the world can't be reconciled with the existence of an all-loving, all-powerful God. It is reasoned that if God were all-loving and all-powerful he'd be willing and able to put an end to suffering. The fact that suffering continues in the world is proof, so it is thought, that an all-loving, all-powerful God does not exist.

Some people attempt to get around this 'riddle' by proposing that God is all-loving but not all-powerful. They say that God—whether by inability or by choice—cannot raise the world above the mess that it is in; that he himself is somehow caught in the trap like the rest of us, and that he is on a journey through the pain. This certainly solves the intellectual problem, since in answer to the question, 'Why doesn't God end all the pain?', this view states: "Because he can't; he, too, is enveloped by the pain of the world". There is a half-truth here. One of the extraordinary things about the biblical portrait of God is that he does experience the pain of this world, and I'll talk more about that later. The problem with this way of thinking—called 'process theology'—is that it sidesteps a fundamental conviction of the Bible. As the Creator of everything, God does govern all things: he is in fact the 'Almighty'.

So, you see, for anyone who adopts a vaguely biblical approach to the question, the dilemma remains. Does the existence of suffering disprove the existence of an all-powerful and all-loving God? Let me put the problem again as a kind of equation:

Assumption 1: An all-powerful God would be able to end suffering.

Assumption 2: An all-loving God would desire to end suffering.

Fact: Suffering exists.

Conclusion: An all-powerful, all-loving God, therefore, does not exist.

The argument has popular appeal and has come to have the 'ring' of truth about it, but in terms of sheer logic it is not all that successful. In academic circles, this argument was refuted centuries ago, and again more recently by leading philosopher, Dr. Alvin Plantinga, Professor of Philosophy at the University of Notre Dame in the U.S.[1] The conclusion *God does not exist* is by no means a logical deduction from the phenomenon of suffering. The existence of suffering could be used as evidence against God's existence only if you could first prove that an all-loving God does not have good reasons for allowing suffering to continue. In other words, the problem in the above equation is Assumption 2 and, in particular, in the words 'would desire'. Until we could show categorically that there

1. A Plantinga, *God and Other Minds: a study of the rational justification of belief in God*, Cornell University Press, London, 1990.

could not be loving purposes behind the continuation of suffering, the logical force of the argument dissolves, even though its emotional force remains. Thus, ironically you could restate the equation to promote an entirely different, though equally reasonable, conclusion:

Assumption 1: An all-powerful God exists.

Assumption 2: An all-loving God exists.

Fact: Suffering exists.

Conclusion: God must have loving reasons (which he is able to achieve) for permitting suffering.

Now, this is not a proof *for* God, of course. I am simply trying to show that whether or not one accepts the argument that suffering disproves God's existence depends not on logic *per se* but on the assumptions with which one comes to the problem. And assumptions are tricky things to validate.

Please don't misunderstand me. I am not for a moment suggesting this settles the problem of suffering. It doesn't even come close. I am just pointing out that the presence of suffering in the world presents not so much an intellectual dilemma for faith in God but an emotional one. The real question of suffering is not, 'Could a god co-exist with a suffering world?' but 'Why would God allow it?' and 'What has he done about it?' These are the more important and more difficult questions I want to pursue in this short book.

Let me begin then by outlining the comprehensive explanations of suffering proposed by the great alternative world traditions of Hinduism, Buddhism, Islam and Atheism. Again, I should say that I have no intention of attempting to *disprove* any of these world views. The questions I will raise about them concern not the truthfulness or otherwise of these religions, but simply the implications of them, if true, for our struggle with suffering. The central goal here is not a critique but a comparison with the perspective found in the Bible.

2

The alternatives

Suffering as balance

All human societies have known suffering and evil. Thus, all major worldviews have had to come to grips with the resulting questions. Hinduism, the oldest of the world's 'formal' religions, has a very clear understanding of the issue. Suffering is explained essentially as pay-back or, perhaps less crudely, as *balance*. Every experience of suffering—famine, disease, rape, earthquake, poverty and so on—is understood to be the operation of 'karma', the universal principle by which all actions of the past are balanced out by events in the present.

Thus, when a three-month-old baby dies in a devout Hindu home, the members of the family sincerely believe the event to be an appropriate 'reaping' in the present of the evil actions sown by family members in the past, whether in this life or in a previous one. (Hindus, of course, believe that all living beings are reincarnated in bodily form until one's individual *karma* allows one to escape physical existence and attain *nirvana*.) Again, when a Hindu woman looks upon a leprous or 'untouchable' man begging in the streets, she will interpret the situation not as an awful inversion of the Creator's intention for the person, but as a divinely sanctioned re-establishment of balance, a pay-back for the man's previous actions. This is not for a moment to imply that Hindus refuse to lend their suffering neighbours a helping hand—Hindus are no less humane than Western materialists, which may or may not be saying a lot—it is simply describing how, philosophically speaking, Hinduism explains the phenomenon of suffering.

There is in Hinduism, therefore, a wonderfully comprehensive account of suffering and evil. The 'Why?' question receives an instant and all-encompassing reply: 'Because it is deserved'. And if in a particular case it does not appear to be deserved, this (so it is explained) is simply because we do not know what evil deeds one has committed in a previous life.

There are, of course, Western and so-called 'Christian' versions of the 'balance' view of suffering. I once met a woman in a country pub who had been devastated by the recent loss of two family members in a car-train collision. She put it down to God's revenge. She had left her husband for another man, and then left that one for yet another. Now God was getting her back, she insisted. I tried to explain that, as far as I could work out, pay-back as she was describing it was a concept quite foreign to the biblical perspective on suffering. But nothing would change her mind. As far as she was concerned, God was angry with her, and that's all there was to it.

Intellectually, the 'balance' view of suffering is quite

satisfying and virtually impossible to disprove. It accounts for every plane crash, every cancer, every bankrupt business. The question that remains for me, though, is an emotional or existential one: If I were to accept that my suffering is a divinely sanctioned balance for my wrongs, is it possible to find consolation in my pain? At one level, comfort may be found in the thought that some of my prior sins have been balanced out, and that therefore one experience of deserved suffering is out of the way. How comforting this will actually be to a mother grieving the loss of her child, or a husband reeling from his wife's betrayal, and so on, I cannot say. And, in any case, this may be an unfair question to ask of Hinduism since, as I understand it, this venerable philosophy is not framed in order to bring comfort to the sufferer. As strange as it may sound to us, comfort for our 'existential angst' is, except for one or two ancient exceptions, a relatively modern spiritual aspiration. Ancient religions were far more concerned with *explanation*, *duty*, *morality* and *ritual* than with *satisfaction for the soul*. Hinduism, then, does not attempt to appeal to the modern Western fixation with consolation; it concerns itself more with an explanation of the phenomenon of suffering itself, and to this extent it succeeds.

Another distinguished tradition from the East, however, takes us down a very different route.

Suffering as an illusion

Like no other religion, Buddhism developed in direct response to the problem of evil and pain. Siddhartha Gautama, later known as the 'Buddha' (or Enlightened One), was the Prince of a region near the present-day borders of Nepal and India (probably around 500BC). After living a somewhat sheltered palace life, at 29 Siddartha ventured out into the world and was immediately struck by three examples of human misery: an "aged man as bent as a roof gable", a "sick man, suffering and very ill, fallen and weltering in his own excreta", and finally a dead body. On returning to the palace he decided to devote the rest of his life to understanding suffering. He promptly left his wife and new-born child, and embarked on a search for answers.

After seven years of rigorous ascetic life, depriving himself of all worldly luxuries, he still did not understand the origin and meaning of pain. And so, in his frustration, so the account runs, he determined to meditate day and night under a Bo Tree (*Ficus religiosa*) until he gained the insight which had eluded him. That moment came one night under a full moon in the month of May. In words attributed to Siddhartha: "My mind was emancipated… Ignorance was dispelled; knowledge arose; darkness was dispelled, light arose". The brilliant and complex understanding of suffering which he acquired suggests, in short, that all pain is an *illusion* through which we must train ourselves to see. Let me explain.

Under the tree, the Buddha came to believe that

our experience of suffering was intimately related to our *desire* or *affection* for the things of the world. For instance, the pain of losing my father was caused not by the crash itself, but by the *affection* I felt for my father. The anguish felt by a beggar is caused not so much by the circumstance of poverty itself, but by the beggar's *desire* for a better life. If the grieving child or the beggar were able to remove their desires for such things—by adopting the path of Buddhism—the experience of pain and suffering would evaporate like the passing of the morning dew; it would be shown to be a mere illusion.

Philosophically, the Buddha's insight is profound. There is little question that our experience of suffering is related to desire. If I desire a full stomach, starvation will feel like suffering; if I desire human intimacy, being widowed will appear to be a tragedy; if I desire wealth, bankruptcy will look like a misfortune, and so on. Remove these desires, and all such feelings dissipate.

Yet, for all its philosophical sophistication, viewing human misery as illusory raises for me a question: Can I live this way? Can a boy faced with the violent death of his father negate his feelings of sorrow, insecurity, love and rage and still be a normal boy living in the real world? I do not know the answer to that question, but I suspect a devout Buddhist might reply that it is precisely the goal of Buddhism to escape (what I call) the 'real world', to experience an emancipation from existence into 'non-existence', or *nirvana*.

A doubt similar to my own was expressed by

the famous *Haiku* (short verse) poet and Buddhist, Kobayashi Issa (1763-1827). Born into poverty, Issa's life was full of misery. He lost his mother at a young age, was ill-treated by his step-mother, lost four of his own children in infancy, and then watched his wife die in childbirth. Nevertheless, by the end of his life he had composed over 20,000 poems and had become (and remains) one of Japan's best loved *Haiku* masters. One of his poems directly addresses the tension he felt between his devout beliefs as a Buddhist and his profound experience of pain. His religious master had instructed him on the necessity of perceiving all earthly circumstances as 'dew', a watery and momentary apparition without real substance. Yet at the death of one of his infant daughters he composed these few, anguished lines:

Tsuyu no yo wa
tsuyu no yo nagara
sari nagara

This world of dew
is only a world of dew—
and yet, and yet.

From a Buddhist perspective, I suspect Issa's final line points to his lack of enlightenment, his inability to see misery for what it was—an illusion. Nevertheless, it does raise the question: How many of us could possibly attain to Siddhartha Gautama's high ideal?

Suffering as determined

A thousand years after the birth of Buddhism, the Middle East would witness the rise of one of the most powerful social movements in the history of the world, the religion of *Islam*, a word which translates as 'submission' (to the will of God). Unlike Buddhism, Islamic thought—codified most authoritatively in the *Koran*—did not arise in particular response to human misery, so its treatment of the topic is far more cursory. Nevertheless, a clear and comprehensive answer to the question of suffering is offered. For the Muslim ('one who submits' to God), all events in history are absolutely determined: from the falling of a leaf, to the trajectory of an asteroid, all of it is controlled by the will of Allah. Events which cause suffering, therefore, such as a plane crash, a war, a deformed baby and so on, are the direct result of the specific finger of the Almighty.

Historically speaking, Muslims hold this view because, quite unlike other Middle Eastern faiths like biblical Judaism and Christianity, Islamic theology was heavily influenced by the thinking of the great Greek philosopher, Aristotle. Indeed, Arabs are often credited with preserving for the world the writings of this most famous student of Plato. Early Jews and Christians, by contrast, appear to have been quite uninterested in the sophisticated Aristotelian worldview. Aristotle, in describing 'God', coined the phrase the 'Unmoved-Mover'. That is, God *moves* all events in the universe but is himself moved by nothing. He causes all effects but is affected by no cause—if you know what I mean!

Islamic theory reflects this view of God in a rigorous and highly developed way. While Allah himself is never 'moved' by anything in the world, anything that 'moves' in the world is moved by Allah. Strictly speaking, this is not 'determinism' since that philosophy tends to attribute all effects to fixed and impersonal causes, whereas Muslims insist that Allah is a highly personal and involved being. It is a potent and compelling point of view, in my opinion.

Marie, a good friend from church, was telling me recently about her firsthand experience of this dimension of Islamic philosophy. She and two girlfriends had been travelling around Turkey during the holy month of Ramadan, when one day at sunset in the middle of the city of Ankara they accidentally locked the keys in the car. Within minutes a crowd of very interested men were gathering around the car—a frightening experience in any city! With the sun going down, and the girls surrounded, they were concerned to say the least. Luckily, they learned of a motor mechanic nearby and so pleaded with him to help them get the keys out of the car. "I am afraid I cannot", he replied, "For it is the will of Allah that the keys are in there". Now, Marie assures me he was deadly serious, but I can't help thinking he was just your typical bloke, either too lazy to get off his backside to help, or looking to create a good story to laugh about later with his mates. All the same, the story does illustrate—perhaps only humorously—something quite central to the Muslim outlook: namely, that all things in the universe are caused by the explicit will of Allah.

The seriousness with which some Muslims take this notion of the 'Finger of Allah', however, is illustrated for me in a not-so-humorous investigation into the events of a *Silk Air* plane crash. On December 19th, 1997, the *Silk Air* Boeing 737 plunged into the Musi River in Indonesia, killing all 104 passengers and crew. The circumstances were suspicious to say the least. Shortly before the crash, Captain Tsu Ming Way, was heard to say that he was going to the cabin, leaving the first officer, New Zealander Duncan Ward, at the controls. A short time later the plane's digital flight data recorder was mysteriously disconnected and within minutes the aircraft was sent into a death dive. According to a report in the *Sydney Morning Herald*, officials in Singapore (where the airline is based) strongly suspect that Captain Tsu, who hated New Zealander pilots (it's a long story!) and who had gambling problems, disconnected the recorders, murdered the first officer with the cockpit fire axe and proceeded to commit suicide by deliberately crashing the aircraft. As if the tragedy were not enough, the *Herald* reports the concern of Singaporean 'sources' that the "strong Muslim beliefs of the chief investigator of the Indonesian National Transportation Safety Committee (NTSC), Professor Oetarjo Diran, could prejudice a finding of pilot suicide as the single cause of the crash". Professor Diran, who concedes the "disturbing and unusual" circumstances of the crash, "does not want relatives of the victims receiving insurance monies from an event that was the will of Allah", the *Herald* reported. Indeed, Diran is alleged to have stated: "if today is your day to die, so be it… it is not proper to claim for God's will".

The point here is not that Muslims reject all forms of compensation, nor that they make for bad accident investigators—I suspect this story was newsworthy precisely because it is not the norm in Indonesia or anywhere else. I refer to it because it highlights an important conviction of classical Islamic theology: the finger of Allah determines all things, even a suicide-murder such as that on December 19th, 1997. To quote A Yusuf Ali, the Muslim scholar whose commentary supplements the *Koran* on my bookshelf, "in Quranic language all consequences are ascribed to God, the Cause of Causes".

The reasons Allah should determine that a plane should crash or a baby be deformed or a war break out are, of course, unknowable and, indeed, unquestionable. To an outsider this may seem a hard pill to swallow, but for the Muslim this is both logical and meaningful. It is logical because the ways of the Almighty are, by definition, beyond the comprehension of our small human minds. It is meaningful because, for the Muslim, the cause of suffering is therefore found not in any factor external to God, such as the doctrine of *karma* in Hinduism or philosophizing about 'desire' in Buddhism, but in the personal activity of the Sovereign God. Suffering thus becomes an opportunity for the faithful to 'submit' (true to the meaning of *Muslim*) to Allah's indisputable will, and to reaffirm the central creed that Allah is the 'Cause of all causes'. To question Allah at this point—to cry out to him 'Why God?'—is to refuse submission and, therefore, to miss the stunning simplicity of Islamic life.

Suffering as natural

Different from all of these perspectives on suffering is the completely non-religious explanation found in *atheism*— the conviction that there is *no God* (*a* = 'no'; *theos* = 'God'). For the atheist, suffering is not the result of *karma* or desire or Allah: it is just natural, the unhappy by-product of a universe driven only by the random intersection of time and space. Everything that happens in the world— whether good or bad—happens without any design and without any thought of us at all. Perhaps the best known proponent of such a view is the Oxford University writer, Richard Dawkins. On the question of suffering, Dawkins has stated with quite 'religious' confidence:

> In a universe of blind physical forces and genetic replication, some people are going to get hurt, other people are going to get lucky, and we won't find any rhyme or reason in it, nor any justice. The universe we observe has precisely the properties we should expect if there is at the bottom no design, no purpose, no evil, and no good; nothing but blind, pitiless indifference. DNA neither knows, nor cares. DNA just is, and we dance to its music.[2]

2. 'The Evolution of the Darwin Man', published during 2000 in *The Sydney Morning Herald*.

In other words, terrible events such as the devastation of an earthquake, the rape of a young woman, or the growth of a malignant cancer emerge as the inevitable consequences of 'chance' or, in Dawkins' more colourful phrase, "blind, pitiless indifference".

Actually, I suspect Dawkins, like a good preacher, is deliberately overstating his case in order to make his point more clear. As a devout atheistic evolutionist— remember, there are plenty of *theistic* evolutionists, who think evolution itself is a work of the Creator—Richard Dawkins does not really believe there is no "rhyme" in the universe, nor does he think evolution is completely "blind". Indeed, one of his contributions to the popularisation of evolutionary theory has been to correct the misconception that evolution implies utter randomness. What we observe in the biological world, he insists, is a clear tendency to 'select' those variations (genetic mutations) that are advantageous to the preservation or progress of a species and to 'reject' those that hinder such survival. The very phrase 'natural *selection*' assumes that there is a pattern—or 'rhyme'—to the process of evolution. This pattern has no Designer behind it as far as atheists are concerned. It is all the result of the wonderful self-governing properties of this 'dot' in the universe we call earth.

Thus far in my account of atheistic evolutionism, Dawkins would say a hearty 'Amen!' or perhaps 'Hear! hear!' The full implications of such a view for the human need to comprehend suffering, however, have not, as far as I know, been explored by Dawkins.

Perhaps this is because he thinks it wise to stick to his area of expertise.

Nevertheless, a major question emerges in my mind as I ponder an atheistic evolutionary account of the problem of pain and suffering: could I live in the midst of a world of pain truly believing that behind it all there is no reason, no design and no pity? I don't doubt that one could maintain the position *intellectually*, particularly if one never experienced pain; but in the midst of real suffering can it be maintained *existentially*, that is, while carrying on a meaningful existence?

Perhaps this is best illustrated in a conversation I heard recounted by a theistic philosopher some years ago. He and an atheist philosopher had been invited to engage in a large public debate on the question of the significance of God's existence. During the course of the debate the atheist insisted that since all events in the universe are random and mindless, the pursuit of questions of meaning in suffering was itself meaningless and irrational. The other responded that such a view lacked empirical credibility since one could not possibly live out such a creed in the real world. Men and women faced with profound injustices or misery have always (and probably will always) cry out 'Why?' Such questions, he argued, appear to be a necessary consequence of our nature as self-aware beings. At the time, the two philosophers begged to differ. That is, until a year or so later when they met again in a more private setting. It turns out that several months after the initial debate, the 'unbelieving' philosopher had lost his daughter in a terrible rape-murder. He now confided in his former opponent that despite his intellectual commitment to atheism, when his daughter was killed he found himself unable to resist the impulse to cry out 'Why?' In his head, atheism seemed reasonable enough; in his experience, it collapsed. The thought that his daughter's life had been lost to a universe of "blind, pitiless indifference", to use Dawkins' phrase, was unbearable and unlivable.

The atheist may be right about God: I do concede the possibility that this grand universe is a monumental fluke (just as I am willing to concede the possibility that you are all aliens sent to earth to study me!). But my point here is that a naturalistic view of evil and suffering provides a framework for human life that is unworkable. To put it succinctly and perhaps rather strangely, if atheism's account of human life is true, it cannot consistently be lived.

By contrast, the biblical perspective seems to me both true and livable, and it's to this that I want now to turn.

3

Invitation to doubt

I should repeat that my own view is not that the Bible presents a crystal clear account of evil and pain, nor that it has some knock-down argument which silences our questions. Far from it. One of the distinguishing things about the Good Book's approach is that it stops short of providing a single, all-governing answer such as that found in Hinduism ('balance') or in Atheism ('natural'). To some, I imagine this will be frustrating. Those that prefer life in streamlined form will probably be attracted to other points of view. But for me there's something about the tension and complexity of the Scriptural perspective on suffering that rings true to the real world, and that leaves me intrigued, stimulated, and above all comforted. Like a great rock song—as opposed to a formulaic pop song—the Bible offers a rhyme, rhythm, ambience and climactic anthem that surprises you each time you listen to it. At least, that has been my experience.

Though I've listened to this biblical 'tune' for quite some years now, as I said earlier this does not mean that I have ceased to ask: "Why, God?" At times I am deeply perplexed by God's dealings in the world. It used to worry me that questioning like this offended the Almighty, that it was a sign of a lack of faith in him. After all, aren't the faithful meant to say things like the words immortalised in Psalm 23: "The Lord is my Shepherd; I shall not want"? Isn't that the kind of trust God demands? Yes, and no!

One of the most striking elements of the Bible's treatment of suffering is the way it endorses our right to question God, to plead with him for some kind of response to our predicament. In fact, rather paradoxically, the psalm immediately before Psalm 23 opens with a cry of doubt you'd expect from the pen of a skeptic rather than a believer. But in fact both psalms may well have had the same composer. Psalm 22 begins:

> My God, my God, why have you forsaken me?
> Why are you so far from saving me,
>   so far from the words of my groaning?
> O my God, I cry out by day, but you do
>   not answer,
>   by night, and am not silent.
>   PSALM 22:1-2

If I were a Buddhist, this sort of questioning would indicate my *un*enlightenment; if I were a Muslim, it would border on blasphemy; if I were an atheist, of course, it would be meaningless. Actually, I suspect most church folk of today would feel uncomfortable repeating the sentiments of this psalm. Sometimes we in the church feel we must declare "The Lord is my shepherd" even if the Shepherd seems to have gone walkabout. But faith isn't like that, at least biblical faith isn't like that. Faith is not the denial of reality, nor does it involve repeating a mantra to dispel the doubts. The presence of Psalm 22 in the Bible, right before Psalm 23, reminds us that we have God's permission to express our disappointment. The true God is One you may surely doubt. He is big enough never to be over-whelmed by your anger or surprised by your questions. Whatever pains or injustices you've experienced or wit-nessed, we are invited to join with the biblical poet in asking, "Why have you forsaken me?"

The same sentiment of doubting faith or, perhaps better, faithful doubting, is found in a modern-day 'psalm'. In one of U2's songs from the album *All That You Can't Leave Behind*, Bono, the lead singer, vents his deep frustration that despite the Christmas-time refrain "peace on earth" (a phrase taken from the biblical Luke 2:14), the world appears light years from true peace. Given all the sorrow and pain, how can we keep singing about peace on earth? Bono finds that the words are "sticking in my throat".

A song like this will disturb some of the faithful. They'll take it as evidence that U2 have 'fallen from grace', that they no longer affirm the faith for which they were once famous. Far be it from me to defend the faith of rock stars, but it seems to me these words simply echo the mood of some of the biblical psalms with their cries and questions to God. Interestingly, Bono was the celebrity chosen to write the introduction to a contemporary edition of the Book of Psalms in a controversial series of published biblical books. In his 'essay' he refers to the psalms, and to Psalm 22 in particular, as the original 'blues' music: "That's what a lot of the psalms feel like to me", he writes, "the blues. Man shouting at God—'My God, my God, why hast thou forsaken me? Why art thou so far from helping me?'" The insight is a good one, but it doesn't quite go far enough. Psalm 22 is not just "man shouting at God", it is God inviting us to do so. By including this psalm (and many like it) in the 'Holy Scriptures', biblical faith adopts a stance quite unlike the comprehensive, doubt-dispelling perspectives on suffering found in other religious traditions. The God of the Bible bids us to approach him with our doubts, our fears and our frustrations. For it is precisely in this mode of personal engagement—"man shouting at God", to borrow Bono's words—that God whispers back his rather unexpected reply.

It is to some of these 'whispers' that we now turn.

But first, a word about my aims. Just as I have not attempted to *dis*prove any of the religious traditions thus far mentioned, I have no particular intention of trying to *prove* the biblical one. The faith of the Bible is so widely misunderstood and misrepresented today that the greater hurdle for a writer like me is not evidence (or lack of it) but misconceptions (and loads of them). In offering a concise explanation of the biblical account of suffering I hope to remove some of these misconceptions and leave the way open for you, the reader, to investigate the truthfulness of biblical faith at your leisure. I have slowly learnt over the years that there are no questions one could possibly put to biblical faith that have not been comprehensively answered—at any level one requires—by some academic in some book on the back shelf of some library. 'Evidence', 'proof', 'argumentation' and the like, appear to be the particular fixations of scholars with biblical faith, so I encourage you to pursue such questions in whatever way you feel comfortable. A list of such books, with a brief description of each, can be found on page 71.

4

The justice of God

The tyranny of the will

Growing up in Sydney, one of my very good friends was an amazingly enthusiastic bloke named Charles. He and I would often spend afternoons sitting up the back of the grandstand at our local soccer oval plotting our world take-overs: I was going to play soccer for Australia and he was going to be a great athlete. Obviously, I failed my ambition, but he nearly achieved his. After high school he devoted himself passionately to running. He moved to Kenya where he worked as a PE teacher and trained under a former marathon champion. He made intermittent trips back to Sydney. On one of his return visits we caught up for coffee and talked about old times and, of course, about running and his ambition one day to make it to the Olympics. I'd never seen him so driven, so seemingly invincible!

He returned to Kenya shortly afterwards and within months he was dead—found fully clothed in bed in his Nairobi flat with froth coming out of the mouth. On the face of it, it appeared as if Charles might have ended his own life by a massive drug overdose—a huge cocktail of drugs was found strewn across the coffee table in the living room. Other factors suggest otherwise. Charles had had a Kenyan girlfriend whose brothers were less than impressed with their sister going out with a white boy. This caused some friction. In addition, the brothers were involved in the Nairobi drug trade, and Charles had been quite protective of his girlfriend against them. This, combined with the fact that Charles was known to have been in good spirits at the time, makes the conclusion of suicide problematic, especially since evidence in the flat indicates that Charles had had visitors that evening. The evidence was noted but not deemed significant. The Nairobi police didn't even bother to use gloves at the scene, and they made no effort to determine who the 'visitors' were. Charles' friends and family will never know the truth, though his mum and dad are adamant: Charles was murdered.

Whatever the truth about Charles' tragic death, it hardly needs saying that so much of the evil and suffering experienced in our world results from human decisions, from the potent reality of our *will*. I'm thinking of the bloodshed and injustice in Yemen, the ongoing terrorism and reprisals in the Middle East or, closer to home, the thousands of muggings, rapes and murders reported every year in Australia. I'm thinking, of course, about my mate, Charles. Less dramatically, I'm thinking of the way I find it so easy to spend $60 on buying myself take-away and so difficult to spend the same amount on relief for the developing world. Somehow, for all the wondrous glimpses of 'goodness'

I see in society, there remains for me the unmistakable stain of selfishness, violence and greed.

Without giving us precise details, the poet who composed Psalm 22 puts part of his suffering down to this tyrannous power of the human will. In the rather unflattering language of an oppressed person, the poet describes his attackers as animals:

> Many bulls surround me;
>   strong bulls of Bashan encircle me.
> Roaring lions tearing their prey
>   open their mouths wide against me...
> Dogs have surrounded me;
>   a band of evil men has encircled me,
>   they have pierced my hands and my feet.
> I can count all my bones;
>   people stare and gloat over me.
> They divide my garments among them
>   and cast lots for my clothing.
>
> PSALM 22:12-13, 16-18

The propensity to injustice, violence and pride so evident in these words has marked human cultures for as long as anyone knows. In fact, according to the biblical account, the arrogance of the human will found expression in the very first human beings. Now, regardless of whether you think that Adam and Eve were historical individuals (and scholars disagree about such matters), the argument of the Bible's opening chapters is very clear. In striking imagery, Genesis 1-3 makes the point that human beings, from the very beginning, misused their divinely sanctioned *independence* as rational beings and sought to become *autonomous*, that is, a *law unto themselves*, without reference to the Creator. The centre of this beautiful yet tragic story puts it this way:

> When the woman saw that the fruit of the tree was good for food and pleasing to the eye, and also desirable for gaining wisdom, she took some and ate it. She also gave some to her husband, who was with her, and he ate it.
>
> GENESIS 3:6

So began the long and tortuous story of the human will: men and women, made in God's image, defying their Maker for an imagined personal gain. When you think about it, this first act of defiance is played out every day in the lives of each one of us: every time we tread on someone else to get where we're going in life, every time we withhold resources from the poor, every time we pursue illicit pleasure instead of marital faithfulness, every time we retaliate when threatened, and so on. And the result? A society scarred with the tyranny, betrayal, poverty and violence we see around us.

But all this raises a question for some: why does God not simply override our wills when we aim to cause harm or offense, and so stop the pain we cause each other? Surely as the God of all the world he has the power to do that? Why doesn't he just step in and stop us making such evil and destructive choices?

The best way to respond to this question is with another question: If God did step in to bend our wills every time we mistreated one another, would the world, in fact, be a better place? At one level the answer is, of course, 'yes'. We wouldn't be fighting each other, we would be generous, and so on. But at the more profound level, the answer must be 'no'. If God intervened each time a crook pulled the trigger of a gun, every time a husband thought about betraying his wife, every time a woman withheld money from the poor, or any other large or small ill-intentioned act of the will, would this improve our quality of life? Only at the superficial level. If God did consistently impose his will over and against our own, wouldn't we accuse God himself of tyranny? It would reduce human dignity to that of a computer or robot; pre-programmed, with no expression of its own. The Almighty would indeed have a world of peace and harmony but we ourselves would have no 'quality of life' to speak of, for we would not be truly living.

This point was illustrated well in the 1998 film *The Truman Show*. Truman is the unknowing subject of a huge television show, set in a small but delightful town he knows as home. From birth he has grown up unaware that those he thinks are his friends, work colleagues and even his wife are, in fact, merely actors, and that his entire life is being secretly filmed and telecast live to millions of viewers around the world. Standing behind the show is Christof, the executive producer, who orchestrates absolutely everything, from the

conversations Truman has in bed at night with his wife
to the weather he experiences in the town. The result
for Truman is an existence without risk, with little sorrow and no harm. If anything threatens to go wrong,
Christof steps in and removes the possibility.

At first, those of us watching the film love the
thought of Truman's existence. We almost wish we could
live there in a world free of risk, danger and trauma. The
turning point in the film comes, however, when Truman
begins to catch on that something is not right. He
notices people acting strangely, he accidentally bumps
into some of the TV crew and so on. Eventually, Truman
realises that his entire life is a monumental set-up. And
so he tries to escape. To cut a long and brilliant story
short, by the end of the film Truman's dramatic and pas-
sionate attempt to flee from the cool, calculated manip-
ulation of the executive producer has us all cheering
from the sidelines. We find ourselves longing for his free-
dom. Even though escaping from the TV set will thrust
Truman into the real world—a world of risk, danger,
pain and sorrow—at least it will be the *real* world, not
some carefully orchestrated sham.

There are times when I wish God would bend
human wills—not mine of course, just those of the
'bad' people!—but in my more rational moments, as I
think through the implications of this, it dawns on me
that if God acted more like the executive producer in
The Truman Show we would have a profound dilemma
on our hands. True, we wouldn't be here pondering,
"Why does a loving God permit evil and suffering?", for

there wouldn't be any, but we would be here asking the more difficult and more tragic question: "Why has God made us like this—without a will, without true personal expression?" The point is purely hypothetical, of course, since a god like this would not allow us to pose such questions. He would 'correct' our thoughts and keep us in the dark, adding to the depth of the tragedy in which we would exist.

But the reality is, God is not portrayed in the Bible as playing 'dolls-house' with the world. We are real independent beings designed for relationship with the Creator, but because of this we are capable also of defiance. Much of the suffering we experience in the world is a direct result of this God-given independence being turned to ill-effect, being turned into autonomy.[3] And so we are able to say *No* to the ways of the Maker: *No* to justice and peace; *No* to marital faithfulness; *No* to sharing resources with the poor; *No* to equal rights for all; *No* to daily human kindness. It is the Garden of Eden all over again and the consequences of it are all too plain.

But this is not to imply that God will forever let us have our own way in the evil expression of our wills.

3. The exact relationship between our independence of will and choice, and God's sovereign will and rule of the world, is not an easy one for us to understand, and I have not tried to delve into its complexities here. For those who want to think further about this, I would recommend Don Carson's excellent book *How long, O Lord* (see p. 73 for details).

The pledge of justice

We look on the Jewish holocaust, the Syrian crisis, the 9/11 attack and so on, and rightly cry out, "Why didn't God do something? Perhaps we should be thankful that God allows us independent expression but once people have acted with evil intent why does he not step in and condemn them?"

The Bible's answer is that he *will* do something; he will step in. He has set aside a day at the end of history when his anger against all the tyrannous acts of men and women will be poured out in full. I am talking about the (in-)famous 'Day of Judgement', a concept misused by rogue preachers and laughed at by misinformed skeptics, but one that has enormous implications for the question of suffering and evil.

The notion of a Judgement Day first emerges in the Old Testament—that part of the Bible written before the time of Christ—but it finds its fullest expression in the teaching of Jesus himself and in the literature that sprang up around him, what we call the New Testament. To give one example from the final book of the Bible, Revelation:

> Then I saw a great white throne and the one who was seated on it. Earth and sky fled from his presence, and there was no place for them. And I saw the dead, great and small, standing before the throne, and books were opened. Another book was opened, which is the book of life. The dead were judged according to

what they had done as recorded in the books.

REVELATION 20:11-12

The language is deliberately ominous, metaphorical and 'apocalyptic' but its point is clear. God, we're told, knows the deeds of "great and small" alike as if recorded in a book, and will one day open the records and *right* all the wrongs.

For all its apparent doom and gloom, the biblical teaching about the Day of Judgement is not a mere theological scare tactic designed to make us more religious. It is, in fact, God's pledge to wounded humanity that he hears their cries for justice, and will one day console them by bringing his justice to bear on every evil act. Thus, in a strange sort of way, God's judgement is a consequence of his love. It is precisely because God loved the victims of the Jewish holocaust that he pledges to punish the perpetrators of this great evil; it is precisely because he loved the massacred Aboriginal communities of 19th-century Australia that he will vent his anger against those who took part in it; it is precisely because he loved my mate Charles that he will bring his possible attackers to final justice even if they escaped earthly justice. As odd as it sounds, the Bible's teaching about divine judgement brings profound comfort. It reminds us that the Creator hears our cries for justice, and will one day console us with a display of loving justice the world has never witnessed.

There is another aspect of God's love seen in the

concept of the Day of Judgement. The God of the Bible is to be distinguished from the capricious gods of ancient Greece or from the strictly just principles of *karma*. He does not 'pay back' every time an injustice is committed—who of us would be standing if that were the case? Instead, he mercifully holds off his judgement, allowing ample opportunity for each of us to experience a spiritual and practical transformation, before he dishes out the full force of his justice. As one New Testament text states:

> The present heavens and earth are reserved for fire, being kept for the day of judgement and destruction of ungodly men. But do not forget this one thing, dear friends: with the Lord one day is like a thousand years, and a thousand years are like a day. The Lord is not slow in keeping his promise [to bring judgement] as some understand slowness. He is patient with you, not wanting anyone to perish, but everyone to come to repentance.
>
> 2 PETER 3:7-9

This judgement is not the last resort because the Almighty is unable or unwilling to exact his justice within history. He has set a Day of Judgement at the end of history precisely because his personality is a unique blend of pure justice mixed with boundless patience, mercy and love.

Thus, God's pledge to console us with his justice

becomes an exhortation to make use of this merciful interval he has allowed before the last resort. For clearly God does not see only the grand acts of evil such as those committed at Myall Creek in the 1800's or in Syria more recently. He sees the evils closer to home: in our own cities, suburbs and homes, and in our hearts. I am glad that the God of the universe intends to right all the wrongs—it's good to know that those who perpetrate evil against others will not escape—but I am also glad that he delays this judgement so that all of us, none of whom are stain-free, can experience the mercy and renewal that lie at the heart of biblical faith.

But this talk about human will and God's pledge of justice resolves only so much. Many more questions remain, some of which I want to approach in the next few sections.

5

The renewal of all things

The disorder of nature

Several years ago a young dad, Nathan, turned up at my church with a question. He had not been to church for years and would never have described himself as a believer. But his beautiful, perfectly healthy 18-month-old girl had just contracted a severe virus of the brain. According to the doctors, she would never walk or talk or feed herself, and she would require hospital care for the rest of her life, however long that may be. His question was: "How could this happen in God's world?" No-one was to blame. There were no evil acts of the will involved. It was nature, not human nature, that had gone seriously wrong on this occasion. What answer is there for someone like Nathan?

As with the issue of the human will, part of the answer is found in the foundational biblical story of the Garden of Eden. In chapter 2, we are deliberately presented with an idyllic picture of creation: the physical environment is a flourishing haven, the first couple are in perfect harmony with each other, and God himself is close at hand, on a conversational basis with them. In other words, the text portrays the world in beautiful imagery as a place of *environmental*, *social* and *spiritual* harmony. By the end of the next chapter, however, each of these three dimensions has been skewed. Adam and Eve are now pointing the blame at each other, God is furious with his beloved creatures and, most significantly for our purposes, the environment itself is said to be "cursed" as a direct result of the actions of the man. In the ensuing speech, the Almighty declares:

> "Because you listened to your wife and ate from the tree about which I commanded you, 'You must not eat of it,'
>> "Cursed is the ground because of you;
>>> through painful toil you will eat of it
>>> all the days of your life.
>> It will produce thorns and thistles for you,
>>> and you will eat the plants of the field.
>> By the sweat of your brow
>>> you will eat your food
>> until you return to the ground,
>>> since from it you were taken;
>> for dust you are,
>>> and to dust you will return."
>
> GENESIS 3:17-19

Unlike so many cultures—including many indigenous peoples—we in Western capitalist societies historically have tended to view the environment as a place of resources, a kind of God-given pantry full of goodies: fields to plow, mineral deposits to mine, beaches to 'resort', and so on. It's as if we have pictured ourselves as somehow separate from the environment, demi-gods sent from heaven, as it were, with a mandate to plunder. In the past 20 years, though, things have dramatically changed as we've realised that our insatiable desire for more energy, more production, and more levels of consumer comfort have led to a significant crisis in the environment (the depletion of the earth's ozone layer being the most obvious example). It has dawned on us that we are not separate from the creation at all, but an integral part of it, and that our actions in the world have real consequences for the environment. Meanwhile, other cultures, particularly indigenous ones, find themselves biting the proverbial lip, resisting the urge to say, "See, I told you. The connection between people and the land must not be underestimated".

I am not suggesting that the biblical and Aboriginal understandings of the land are the same. I am simply drawing attention to the fact that as our society has become more and more industrialised and technologized, we have slowly lost touch with a reality that has been part of the consciousness of most cultures since time began: there is an intimate connection between human beings and the physical environment.

The Bible's peculiar version of this connection is profound and to modern ears a little strange. When humanity defied the Creator, this had devastating consequences for the creation itself. The physical environment—the land, the flora, the fauna, the atmosphere, and so on—fell under the spell of our displacement of God. In the words of Genesis 3 again: "cursed is the ground because of you". A 'curse' is a pronouncement of judgement. Thus, in biblical thought the earth bears the scars, as it were, of the traumatic rift that has occurred between us and God; it contains an ever-present reminder that the Creator is displeased with our defiance of him. From the DNA inside the human body to the tectonic plates under the earth's surface, the physical world now contains a measure of frustration and chaos. Viruses grow out of control, earthquakes decimate, planes fall from the sky. Although there is more than enough beauty and order still left in the creation to remind us that the universe is no fluke, there is enough disorder evident to remind us that things are not as they should be.

This is the Bible's profound account of this 'fallen' natural world. My friend Nathan needed little convincing of this point. What had happened to his daughter was ample evidence that the world was not as it should be. Thus, the biblical perspective answered the intellectual aspect of his question: How could this happen in God's world? But he had a deeper question to reckon with: What, if any, are God's intentions toward this state of affairs?

This too is something the Bible addresses.

The pledge of renewal

Many years ago some dear friends, Marie and Paul, lost their baby girl mid-pregnancy under dreadful circumstances. She was to be their first girl after three fantastic boys. Paul and I went out for coffee at the time, to chat and to try to make sense of the madness. I don't think I was any help at all. I listened, and we swapped stories about how miserable the world appears sometimes. Days later, Paul and Marie and the boys held a memorial service for Kathleen, their daughter known only by name. As their token 'very religious' mate, I was invited to conduct the service down by the water near where we live. It was a very special honour. The council very kindly planted a memorial tree, and as we gathered around this little piece of God's creation—an Aussie paperbark tree—we mourned for the loss and chaos that had entered their lives. I read from the Bible that morning a passage full of honesty, on the one hand, about the sorrows of this created world, and yet hope, on the other, that God intended better things in the future. Here is the passage we read together.

> The creation waits in eager expectation for the sons of God to be revealed. For the creation was subjected to frustration, not by its own choice, but by the will of the one who subjected it, in hope that the creation itself will be liberated from its bondage to decay and brought into the glorious freedom of the children of God.
>
> ROMANS 8:19-21

Here is the flip-side of the Bible's description of the connection between humanity and the physical environment. Not only was the creation damaged by our displacement of God, it will one day be 'set free' as a result of God's liberation of us. As strange as it sounds to our ears, the Bible insists that on the day God rights the moral wrongs of history—the Judgement Day—he will right the environmental chaos as well. In other words, God pledges to renew the physical universe itself.

This is one of the most distinctive elements of the biblical understanding of the future. Eastern traditions such as Hinduism and Buddhism respond to the problem of the disorder of the natural world by holding out the hope of *nirvana* (literally, 'blown-out'), an eternal state of absolute *non*-physicality. For these philosophies, physical reality is not reality at all, but an entrapment from which we must eventually free ourselves. Biblical hope is radically different. When the Good Book describes the future eternal kingdom of God—what we commonly call 'heaven'—it speaks not of the removal of physical existence but of its renewal. The passage just quoted says the *creation itself* will be set free from its bondage to decay.

In fact, the climactic description of that kingdom, found in the final pages of the Bible, speaks not of 'going to heaven' at all, but of heaven coming to earth and transforming everything:

Then I saw a new heaven and a new earth; for the first heaven and the first earth had passed away... I saw the holy city, the new Jerusalem, coming down out of heaven from God, prepared as a bride beautifully dressed for her husband. And I heard a loud voice from the throne saying, "Now the dwelling of God is with men, and he will live with them. They will be his people, and God himself will be with them and be their God. He will wipe every tear from their eyes. There will be no more death or mourning or crying or pain, for the old order of things has passed away". He who was seated on the throne said, "I am making everything new!" Then he said, "Write this down, for these words are trustworthy and true".

REVELATION 21:1-5

For many of us, even for some long-term believers, our picture of the 'kingdom come' derives from an unlikely combination of ancient Greek philosophy and modern Hollywood movies. The ancient Greek philosopher Plato taught that the physical world is a kind of grubby reflection of the ultimate non-physical reality to which everything is headed. Buddhism and Hinduism, with their goal of nirvana, share a similar outlook. Somehow, Hollywood got hold of this idea and now almost always portrays the afterlife as an airy-fairy, fourth-dimensional existence with clouds, halos, bright lights and the ever-present harp music.

In the years after I came to believe in Christ, it always troubled me that I was now meant to enjoy the thought of escaping the physical world and entering a spiritual one called heaven. I loved the taste, smell, sight, sound and touch of this world, and here I was being told to look forward to losing those five senses and having them replaced by a spiritual sixth sense. I was not terribly excited about it. Then someone challenged me to point to biblical texts that describe the afterlife as a disembodied, nirvana-like bliss. I couldn't. Every passage I turned to challenged the Hollywood version of heaven. It turns out that the biblical 'kingdom come' is not an ethereal place of clouds and ghosts, but a tangible place of real existence: it is a 'new creation'. Whether or not we will gain a 'sixth sense' I have no idea, but I think we can count on keeping the other five senses.

This is a future I can get excited about. It is *life* in the fullest sense of the word, a reality in which the moral and physical tensions of our current world will be resolved through an extraordinary act of divine re-creation. And when I find myself doubting that such a fantastic hope could ever become a reality, I need only go down to the beach near where I live or look up at the glorious night sky and remind myself that God has already done it once: the proof is right there before my eyes. Why should I question his ability to do it a second time?

But there is another piece of evidence left in the world by the Almighty to indicate his intention of res-urrecting the physical world itself. It is the resurrection of Christ himself (on the historicity of the resurrection see the books recommended in the list on page 71).

Christ's rising to life is central to biblical faith not merely because it marks out his life as a unique moment in history, but because by it God shows that he is willing and able to breathe new life where there is currently death. The resurrection of Jesus is God's tangible pledge within history that he intends to do the same for the whole creation at the end of history. This current world convinces me of God's *ability* to re-create the universe; the resurrection of Jesus convinces me of his *intention* to do just that.

Nathan, the young father whose 18-month-old girl, Ali, had been struck down by a brain virus, continued his questioning over several months and ended up at the final book of the Bible, and to the passage quoted above in particular. He needed no convincing that the physical world was in chaos; but the news that God has pledged to renew the universe, not merely spiritually but 'bodily', struck him as profound. It convinced him that what he wanted for his daughter was precisely what God had promised—the renewal of nature. This brought a whole new perspective to his life and to his pain. As one who previously had no clearly defined faith he emerged from his questioning with some answers to ponder and a real hope to cling to. I wrote to him while I was preparing for this book and asked him to share his own thoughts on this difficult subject. He emailed straight back these striking lines:

Ali being sick has many positive aspects about it in terms of bringing our family closer together and allowing us to help other children in similar situations, as we have been able to lobby the government and hospitals for changes. It has also enabled us to learn more about Christianity and put some perspective on life.

The most important thing however for us is to know that Ali will pass to the new creation where she will be healthy and able to run and play as a physically normal child. She will feel no pain and will not know or remember any of the current being. We will be there to share this with her and the rest of her family. I also talked to my mother about this as she died with cancer and it was comforting for her.

The final biblical insight into suffering I want to talk about concerns not so much what God will do in the future, but what he has done in the past and how this brings comfort in the present.

6

The wounds of God

For me, the most painful effects of losing my father occurred not at the time of the crash itself when I was just nine, but years later when I was about 18. I remember at that time beginning to watch some of my friends becoming 'mates' with their dads, turning that emotional corner from treating their fathers as the household policeman to someone they now looked up to and wanted to confide in. It came home to me one evening in particular. I was out on the back balcony with one of my best mates, Ben, just chatting about 'stuff'—sport, girls, ambitions, sport, and girls. Ben's dad, Art, someone I already looked up to in a big way, came out with beers in hand. It wasn't the first beer Art had let Ben taste, and it certainly wasn't the first beer Ben had had, but this was different. This was a deliberate father-son moment, a way of saying to Ben, "Now we drink beer together", which in my book back then meant a lot. Of course, Art included me in the little ritual—I think he was always conscious of me in that way—but it wasn't quite the same. Although there was a sense in which we were 'mates', he was not my dad and I was not his son.

The question when I was nine was, "Mum, why did God let Dad's plane crash?" The questions at 18 were different. I had come to accept the claims about Christ during my high school years, and so my doubt and confusion now was that of a believer struggling to fit together my feelings and my faith. I found myself asking: "God, where are you in all this? What could you know about my pain? When have you ever experienced loss?" It was then that I discovered—or rather, had pointed out to me—the most extraordinary contribution of biblical thought to the problem of human pain: God himself has wounds.

I mentioned earlier that in Islamic thought God is seen as the 'Unmoved-Mover', the one who moves everything, but is himself moved by nothing. This is one of the strongest points of contrast between biblical faith and that of the *Koran*, as any Muslim will tell you. At the heart of the Bible's presentation of God is the incredible and unapologetic affirmation that God himself suffers; that he is the 'Deeply-Moved-Mover'.

Just think of the Bible's story-line for a moment. It reads like a classic tragedy: the Creator designs the world to have independent relationship with himself; that independence is turned by us into autonomy as we neglect and reject him; he enters that world in the person of Christ and, once again, is rejected, mocked and brutally executed on a cross; and yet even still, after such a dramatic display of commitment to the world, men and women refuse the advances of the

Almighty. As strange as it sounds, we could well ask, "Who has experienced misery more than the suffering God revealed in the pages of the biblical narrative?"

This dimension of God's story is nowhere more clearly demonstrated than in the crucifixion scene of the Gospel of Mark, the first biography of Christ written shortly after his life. Here the circumstances and cry of the anguished poet who composed Psalm 22, discussed previously, become the very circumstances and cry of Jesus himself. Let me display both texts (on the following page) so you can see what I mean:

PSALM 22

My God, my God, why have you forsaken me? Why are you so far from saving me, so far from the words of my groaning? O my God, I cry out by day, but you do not answer.

In you our fathers put their trust; they trusted and you delivered them. They cried to you and were saved; in you they trusted and were not disappointed.

But I am a worm and not a man, scorned by men and despised by the people. All who see me mock me; *they hurl insults, shaking their heads.*

Dogs have surrounded me; a band of evil men has encircled me, *they have pierced my hands and my feet.* I can count all my bones; people stare and gloat over me. They divide my garments among them and *cast lots for my clothing.*

MARK 15

They put a purple robe on [Jesus], then twisted together a crown of thorns and set it on him. And they began to call out to him, "Hail, king of the Jews!" Again and again they struck him on the head with a staff and spat on him.

And they crucified him. Dividing up his clothes, *they cast lots to see what each would get.*

Those who passed by hurled insults at him. Those crucified with him also heaped insults on him.

And at the ninth hour Jesus cried out in a loud voice, *"Eloi, Eloi, lama sabachthani?"*—which means, *"My God, my God, why have you forsaken me?"* With a loud cry, Jesus breathed his last.

Just as the famous 'blues' poet centuries before Christ had been the object of ridicule and mockery, so those who passed by Jesus hurled insults at him, and those crucified with him did the same. Just as the poet's very garments had been seized by his enemies, so the soldiers at the foot of Christ's cross divided his clothes among themselves and drew straws to see what each would get to take home. Just as the poet could state metaphorically, "they have pierced my hands and my feet", so Jesus experienced real nails the thickness of my finger driven through his hands and feet.

It seems that Mark has deliberately worded his account of Jesus' death to recall the lines of the ancient suffering psalmist. This is not to say Mark made stuff up: gambling for the clothes of a vanquished foe, for instance, was a very common practice in the ancient world, and was likely to have occurred at many public executions. My point is that the first believers perceived in the events of Jesus' crucifixion an uncanny parallel with the lyrics of the psalm that had been sung in many a synagogue service for hundreds of years. More than that, Jesus' cry from the cross made that connection explicit.

In the final moments of his life, as blood loss began to draw away his strength and asphyxiation stole his very breath, Jesus searched for words that would convey to the large crowd of onlookers his innermost feelings. He chose the opening line of Psalm 22, and so that all could hear he cried out, "*Eloi, Eloi, lama sabachthani?*" which is Aramaic (the language of first-century Palestine) for "My God, my God, why have you forsaken me?"

This is not a cry of self-doubt from Christ's lips, as if he is here questioning his identity and mission. It his deliberate and agonizing identification with the suffering poet of Psalm 22 and therefore, with all those who have cried out to God 'Why?' There on the cross, so the Bible insists, God intentionally enters our pain and misery, getting his hands dirty and even bloody. This is God at his most vulnerable and yet at his most glorious.

I once spoke on this theme of *the wounds of God* at Western Sydney University. After the speech, which I felt had gone quite well, the chairperson asked the audience for questions. Without delay a man in perhaps his mid-30's stood up and proceeded to tell the audience how preposterous was the claim that the Creator of the universe should be subjected to the forces of his own creation—that he would have to eat, sleep and go to the toilet, let alone die on a cross. His monologue, which was the longest five minutes of my speaking career, was intelligent, articulate and, for the most part, very civil. He was a Muslim leader at the university and an academic—just my luck. When the chair invited me to respond I did my best to engage his central concerns. We went to and fro for another ten minutes during which he insisted that the notion of God having wounds—whether physical or emotional—was not only illogical, since the 'Cause of Causes' could not possibly be caused pain by a lesser entity, it was an outright blasphemy: texts in the *Koran* say so (for instance, *Sura* 5:19, 75, 76, 78). I had no knock-down argument, no witty comeback. The debate was probably too amicable for either approach anyway. In the end, I simply thanked him for demonstrating for the audience the radical contrast between the Islamic conception of God and that described in the Bible. What the Muslim denounces as blasphemy the Christian holds as precious: God has wounds.

As I've already said, I don't think I have answers for all my intellectual questions about suffering and pain. I guess I could write another book on all the stuff I don't know about suffering. But what I learnt as an 18-year-old, as I was wondering what God understood of my loss, has changed my perspective forever. In the great work of art we call the universe, I cannot always follow the hand of the Artist: some of his work just eludes me. But what the biblical narrative tells me— and, in particular, the account of Christ's passion—is that while I may not be able to trace the Artist's hand at all times, I can always trust his motives. The God who is in control of all things, who acts behind the scenes in all things, is also the God who willingly suffers. He is the one I can shout at, cry with and find comfort in. His heart, if not all his ways, is clear to me because on the cross he wore it on his sleeve for all to see. This God is able to sympathise with those who suffer not simply because he is 'all-knowing'— an attribute ascribed to any version of divinity—but because he has experienced pain firsthand. It's a point captured beautifully in the last stanza of a modern poem called 'Jesus of the Scars' written by Edward Shillito shortly after WWI:

> The other gods were strong; but thou wast weak;
> They rode, thou didst stumble to a throne
> But to our wounds only God's wounds can speak
> And not a god has wounds, but thou alone.

Having said this, God's wounds speak to more than just our wounds, they address something even more fundamental.

The invitation to mercy

Christ's death is more than an identification with us. The Bible makes clear it is a substitution for us. On the cross God not only stands alongside us, he stands in our place. Here we arrive at perhaps the most liberating dimension of biblical faith: in that *godforsaken* moment on the cross Jesus bore the *godforsakenness* I deserve for rejecting my Maker and mistreating my neighbour, or in biblical shorthand, for my 'sin'. Jesus' death, therefore, is God's invitation to experience not just his comfort but his mercy as well.

When I watched the Russell Crowe extravaganza *Gladiator*, some years ago, I followed it up straight away with a behind-the-scenes documentary about the making of the movie. The information is eye-opening.

You discover that the amazing set seen in the film was really just a tiny, computer-enhanced façade. You learn that what appeared like seamless acting throughout came only after hundreds of 'bloopers', the out-takes of which were included in the doco. Best of all, if you're a 'bore' like I am, there were personal interviews with the director where you find out the movie-maker's real motives and meaning behind each scene.

After watching all this, I was reminded of the kind of behind-the-scenes knowledge the Almighty must have of each one of us. You and I look at each other and see just the film, as it were. Some of our films are rather B-grade, admittedly, but on the whole (and on the surface) there doesn't appear to be too much for us to be ashamed of. Yet God sees beyond the surface. He has the total, uncut insight into our lives. He sees through my rather flimsy façade; he knows every one of my regrettable mistakes, and even the ones I should have regretted but didn't; best, or worst, of all, he knows my true motives: that 'good deed' done for show, that kind word said with duplicity. He knows it all.

Yet, through the death of Christ all my shame is transformed into hope—hope that despite my guilt, the God of the universe invites me to enjoy his mercy now. To quote a remarkable passage from the New Testament:

> If anybody does sin, we have one who speaks
> to the Father in our defense—Jesus Christ, the

righteous one. He is the atoning sacrifice for
our sins: and not only for ours but also for the
sins of the whole world.

1 JOHN 2:1-2

On the Day of Judgement, when all the behind-the-
scenes material is revealed, so to speak, and God rights
the wrongs of history, the cross will be my only hope.
I won't be trying to convince the Almighty that I really
was a 'good bloke' after all. I won't be pointing the
finger at all the easier targets—those people who were
worse than I ever was. I'll just be looking to God to
make good on his promise that this Day was delayed
precisely so that those who respond to him during the
merciful interval between creation and 'new creation'
may experience both the forgiveness of 'sins' now and
the renewal of the universe then.

This is why biblical faith speaks so poignantly not
only to those who suffer but to all who know
themselves to be part of this fallen world. But that's for
another book.

Books for further reading

The Essential Jesus, **Matthias Media, 2008.** Contains a fresh translation of the Gospel of Luke (the account of Jesus' life) with some brief background information that explains what happened in the Bible in the lead-up to Luke's Gospel. An excellent place to start if you want to read the words of Jesus for yourself.

Simply Christianity by **John Dickson, Matthias Media, 1999.** Apologies for the shameless self-promotion. If you want a simple, no-nonsense explanation of the life of Christ, this may suit. Alternatively…

Scaling the Secular City by **JP Moreland, Baker Book House, 1987.** In my opinion, this is the best all-round, serious defence of a number of elements of the Christian faith. Not easy going, but worth having on the bookshelf. Deals profoundly with many different questions.

The Truth About Jesus by **Paul Barnett, 2nd edn, Aquila, 2004.** Excellent summary of the historical evidence for Jesus' life, death and resurrection. Easy to read.

A Doubter's Guide to Jesus by John Dickson, Zondervan, 2018. An introduction to Jesus as he is portrayed in the earliest historical sources. Looks at the material in all its diversity, revealing Jesus in all his multi-layered complexity.

A Doubter

Guide to the Bible by John Dickson, Zondervan, 2014. A concise Bible primer summarizing the main themes in Scripture, and addressing questions like 'How can we read the creation account in Genesis in light of modern science?' and 'How do we approach the Old Testament law when it appears inconsistent and irrelevant?' Helps you to see why the Bible has been a compelling, life-changing and magnetic force throughout the ages.

Philosophers Who Believe edited by KJ Clark, IVP, 1993. Professional academic philosophers tell of their own faith in Christ. Excellent for anyone with an interest in philosophical queries about faith.

Darwin On Trial by Phillip E Johnson, 3rd edn, IVP, 2010. An excellent analysis of the scientific doctrine of evolution by natural selection. It is not simple to read because it is not a simplistic treatment. Well thought out and up to date.

Intelligent Design by William Dembski, IVP, 1999. This is a popularisation of the author's academic tome, *The Design Inference,* a work regarded as a watershed in scientific and mathematical modeling for the detection of design (and therefore a Designer) in the universe. The current book is serious but very readable. It offers both a critique of atheism and a presentation of the strengths of theism.

How Long O Lord? by DA Carson, 2nd edn, Baker Book House, 2006. Excellent treatment of the question of suffering. Pitched at people who already believe but offers a more comprehensive theological account of suffering than the one in this book.

Walking with God through Pain and Suffering by Timothy Keller, Penguin Random House, 2013. Deals with the age-old question: How do we deal with pain and suffering both in our own lives and in the world around us? Offers guidance and encouragement to those for whom suffering is not an abstraction but a fact of life.

If I Were God, I'd Make Myself Clearer by John Dickson, 2nd edn, Matthias Media, 2019. With so many religions on offer, can one of them be considered true? Or are they different paths up the same spiritual mountain? If there really is something spiritual out there, wouldn't there be some pretty clear signposts to it? This book considers the vast array of spiritual claims made by different religions and individuals, and asks what clarity can be found.

Christianity On Trial by Colin Chapman, Lion, 1988. Easy to read, all-purpose book. Deals with loads of commonly asked scientific, historical and philosophical questions about faith and provides brief answers.

God and Other Minds by Alvin Plantinga, Cornell University Press, 1990. A series of high-level philosophical essays demonstrating that belief in God is entirely rational. One of the chapters provides a comprehensive answer to the question: Does suffering disprove the existence of God?

Did Jesus Rise From the Dead? The Resurrection Debate by Gary Habermas and Antony Flew, Wipf and Stock, 2003. This is an extraordinary book. On May 2nd and 3rd 1985, the philosophy faculty of Liberty University, Virginia USA, hosted a professionally adjudicated public debate between renowned scholar and atheist Professor Antony Flew and an internationally recognised expert in the origins of Christianity, historian Dr. Gary Habermas. The topic of the debate was 'The Historicity of the Resurrection: Did Jesus Rise from the Dead?' It was attended by 3000 people, and the transcripts of the debate have been published in this book. Read it and make up your own mind about this central aspect of biblical belief.

The Existence of God by Richard Swinburne, 2nd edn, Oxford University Press, 2004. As the title suggests, this is a full-scale demonstration of the existence of God. It is not for the novice, but if you are someone or know someone with high-level intellectual doubts about the reality of God, this is the book to read.

❀matthiasmedia

Matthias Media is an independent Christian publishing company based in Sydney, Australia. To browse our online catalogue, access samples and free downloads, and find more information about our resources (including other books by John Dickson) visit our website:

www.matthiasmedia.com

How to buy our resources
1. Direct from us over the internet:
   – in the US: www.matthiasmedia.com
   – in Australia: www.matthiasmedia.com.au

2. Direct from us by phone: please visit our website for current phone contact information.

3. Through a range of outlets in various parts of the world. Visit **www.matthiasmedia.com/contact** for details about recommended retailers in your part of the world.

4. Trade enquiries can be addressed to:
   – in the US and Canada: sales@matthiasmedia.com
   – in Australia and the rest of the world: sales@matthiasmedia.com.au

Also by John Dickson

Simply Christianity: A modern guide to the ancient faith

One of the reasons people sometimes avoid looking into Christianity is that there are so many versions on offer, each with its own religious package. The project of this book is to get beyond the rituals, myth and dogma. By going back to the earliest biographies of Jesus—the Gospels in the New Testament—*Simply Christianity* finds what remains after the 'religion' is stripped away. It's a great book for understanding the core of Christian faith.

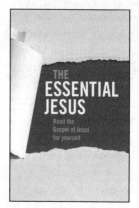